HELEN *Keller*

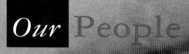

SPIRIT
of America®

HELEN *Keller*

AUTHOR AND ADVOCATE FOR THE DISABLED

By Deborah Kent

Content Adviser: Ken Stuckey, Retired Research Librarian,
Perkins School for the Blind, Boston, Massachusetts

The Child's World®
Chanhassen, Minnesota

7

HELEN *Keller*

Published in the United States of America by The Child's World®
PO Box 326 • Chanhassen, MN 55317-0326 • 800-599-READ • www.childsworld.com

Acknowledgments
The Child's World®: Mary Berendes, Publishing Director

Editorial Directions, Inc.: E. Russell Primm, Editorial Director; Pam Rosenberg, Line Editor; Elizabeth K. Martin, Assistant Editor; Olivia Nellums, Editorial Assistant; Susan Hindman, Copy Editor; Susan Ashley, Halley Gatenby, Proofreaders; Jean Cotterell, Kevin Cunningham, Peter Garnham, Fact Checkers; Tim Griffin/IndexServ, Indexer; Dawn Friedman, Photo Researcher; Linda S. Koutris, Photo Selector

Photo
Cover: Hulton Archive/Getty Images; Courtesy of the American Foundation for the Blind, Helen Keller Archives: 6, 7, 8, 10, 15, 18, 19, 21, 25, 26, 28; Bettmann/Corbis: 9, 11, 12, 14, 20, 22, 23 top and bottom, 27; Corbis: 16; Roger Viollet/Getty Images: 17 bottom; Hulton Archive/Getty Images: 2, 17 top; Courtesy of the Perkins School for the Blind, Watertown, Massachusetts: 13.

Library of Congress Cataloging-in-Publication Data
Kent, Deborah.
  Helen Keller : author and advocate for the disabled / by Deborah Kent.
    p. cm. — (Our people)
"Spirit of America."
Summary: Provides a brief introduction to Helen Keller, her accomplishments, and her impact on American history. Includes bibliographical references and index.
  ISBN 1-59296-005-7 (lib. bdg. : alk. paper)
  1. Keller, Helen, 1880–1968—Juvenile literature. 2. Blind-deaf women—United States—Biography—Juvenile literature. 3. Blind—Civil rights—Juvenile literature. [1. Keller, Helen, 1880–1968. 2. Blind. 3. Deaf. 4. People with disabilities. 5. Women—Biography.] I. Title. II. Series.
  HV1624.K4K46 2003
  362.4'1'092—dc21   2003004179

10   21   28

Contents

Chapter ONE

The Magic of Words

IN 1964, PRESIDENT LYNDON B. JOHNSON awarded the Presidential Medal of Freedom to Helen Keller. This medal is the highest honor the nation can give to a **civilian.** Helen Keller received the Medal of Freedom because she had spent her life in service to others. She worked for world peace, the rights of the poor, and equal rights for women. Above all, she fought to improve the lives of people with **disabilities.** Helen Keller understood disability from the inside. She herself was both blind and deaf.

Helen Keller was awarded the Presidential Medal of Freedom in 1964.

Helen Adams Keller was born on June 27, 1880, in Tuscumbia, Alabama. When she was 19 months old, she fell **gravely** ill. After she got better, Helen's parents made a shocking discovery. Their beloved daughter could no longer see or hear.

When Helen became deaf, she lost what speech she had learned. She couldn't hear people talking and couldn't understand or **imitate** words. When she couldn't ask a question or explain what she needed, she became furious. In her rage she hit, bit, and kicked the people around her. Helen's parents felt very sorry for her. They let her run wild through the house and do whatever she liked. At meals, they even let her snatch food from other people's plates. Helen was like a wild animal because she couldn't communicate her needs.

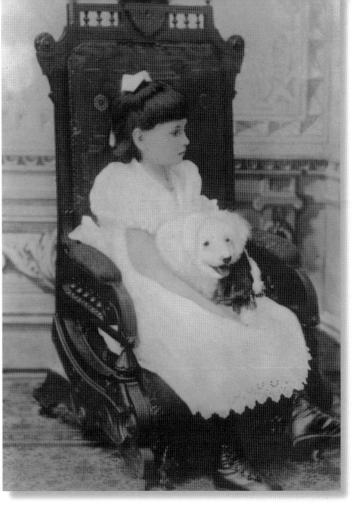

This picture of Helen Keller and her dog was taken in 1887.

7

At last, Helen's parents grew desperate. They wrote to the Perkins Institution for the Blind in Boston, Massachusetts—now the Perkins School for the Blind in Watertown, Massachusetts—asking for help. Michael Anagnos, the director of Perkins, sent one of his recent graduates to teach Helen. The young woman's name was Annie Sullivan. Annie's vision had been poor since she was five years old. When she was 14 an operation restored much of her sight, but her vision was still poor enough for her to go to Perkins.

Annie Sullivan became Helen Keller's teacher when Helen was six years old.

Annie Sullivan reached Tuscumbia in March 1887. On her first day, she began to spell words into Helen's hand, using the manual alphabet for the deaf. Annie spelled

This water pump at Helen Keller's birthplace is the spot where Helen finally understood that everything around her had a name.

as she and Helen ate, played, and went for walks. At first, Helen fought when Annie made her sit still and pay attention. Helen had no idea that Annie's fingers spelled words. She didn't even remember that words existed.

One morning, Annie and Helen stood at the outdoor pump, filling a pail with water. As Annie pumped, Helen felt the fresh, cold water stream over her hand. Annie lifted Helen's hand and spelled W-A-T-E-R against her palm. Suddenly, Helen beamed with

Interesting Fact

▸ When she arrived at the Perkins Institution for the Blind, Helen Keller met 59-year-old Laura Bridgman. Laura was one of the first deafblind people ever to be educated.

Using finger spelling, Annie Sullivan provided Helen Keller with the gift of communication with other people.

excitement. She spelled W-A-T-E-R back to Annie and splashed with her hand. Then she touched a tree, a stone, and a fence. Annie spelled the name of each object, and Helen eagerly spelled it back to her. For the first time, Helen realized that everything around her had a name. She understood that the movements of Annie's fingers in her hand had meaning. Annie Sullivan had unlocked the secret of language for her pupil and given her the means to communicate with others.

ANNIE SULLIVAN COMMUNICATED WITH HELEN KELLER USING THE MANUAL alphabet, a system of finger spelling. Each letter of the alphabet is represented, or shown, by forming the fingers into a particular shape. Finger spelling is used by deaf people, who "read" it by sight. A deafblind person such as Helen Keller "reads" the words by touch when they are spelled directly into the hand. Some scholars believe that finger spelling was invented long ago by European monks who had taken vows of silence. In the 1830s, the method was used at the Perkins Institution for the Blind to teach Laura Bridgman, one of the first deaf-blind students ever to be educated.

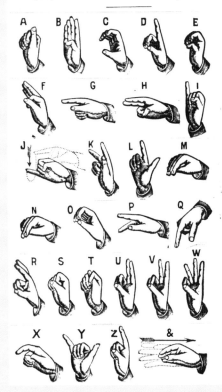

The Deaf and Dumb Alphabet.

Various forms of sign language have been used by many different groups throughout history. In fact, Native Americans living in the Great Plains region had a well-developed system of sign language. This system was used when members of tribes, who spoke different languages, needed to communicate. Today, many deaf people in the United States use American Sign Language to communicate. American Sign Language evolved over the years so that in addition to there being signs for each letter of the alphabet, there are also signs for specific words or common phrases. So many people have become interested in learning American Sign Language that it has become the fourth most used language in the United States.

11

Chapter TWO

The Child Wonder

Horseback riding and other activities helped Helen Keller learn more about the world around her.

HELEN WAS HUNGRY TO LEARN. SHE WANTED to know the name of everything around her. Annie wrote that Helen was "all fingers and curiosity." Soon Helen was spelling full sentences. With her hands, she talked to her teacher and family.

Annie helped Helen learn about the world through her sense of touch. Annie took her swimming and horseback riding. She taught her to climb trees. When the circus came to town, Annie asked the manager to let Helen touch the animals. Helen petted a lion cub and sat on the back of an elephant.

Helen learned to read and write **Braille.** Annie also taught her to write with a pencil. When she was eight, Helen kept a journal. One entry reads: "I read in my books about large fierce animals. Fierce is much cross and strong and very hungry."

After a year in Alabama, Annie took Helen on a long train trip to Boston. Helen enrolled at the Perkins Institution for the Blind. Michael Anagnos was thrilled by Helen's progress. He filled the school's annual reports with news about everything she was doing. Newspapers carried the story, and suddenly Helen Keller was famous.

People wrote to her from all over the country, telling her how much they admired

Helen Keller and Michael Anagnos, director of the Perkins school

Alexander Graham Bell was Helen Keller's lifelong friend.

her. They were amazed by all the things she had learned to do. Helen's success inspired people to try harder in their own lives. She received letters from some of the most important people in the nation. Helen became lifelong friends with Alexander Graham Bell, teacher of the deaf and inventor of the telephone. He knew Helen's father and recommended the Perkins Institution to him. Helen also formed a close friendship with the writer Mark Twain, author of *The Adventures of Huckleberry Finn.* She even met President Grover Cleveland.

Most people imagined that Helen lived in a frightening world of darkness and silence. To Helen, however, the world was not silent and dark. It was rich with smells, tastes, and textures. She knew when someone was coming because she felt the vibrations of footsteps on the floor. The smell of a fresh breeze told her when a window was open. She recognized the hands of nearly everyone she knew.

When she was 10 years old, Helen told Annie that she wanted to learn to speak. Speech was her most difficult challenge. Over the years, many expert teachers worked with her. Little by little, Helen learned to make sounds and form them into words. She worked extremely hard, but her speech never became clear. People had to listen very hard to understand her.

When she was a teenager, Helen Keller spent a lot of time trying to learn how to speak.

Annie Sullivan read many books to Helen by spelling them to her.

In 1896, Helen entered the Cambridge School for Young Ladies. Annie Sullivan sat beside her in class, spelling the teachers' **lectures** into her hand. Only a few of Helen's books were in Braille. Annie read her the others, spelling them page by page. Helen typed her exams so her teachers could read them. She was a fast and **accurate** typist.

Helen had little time for fun. Sometimes she and Annie grew exhausted with the endless work. But Helen was determined to succeed at the Cambridge School. She had decided to do something no deafblind person had ever done before. She had made up her mind to go to college.

16

LOUIS BRAILLE WAS BORN IN 1809 NEAR PARIS, France. At the age of three he injured one of his eyes and an infection developed in the injured eye. The infection spread to the other eye and he was left blind in both eyes. When he was 10 years old, he went to a school for the blind in Paris. There he met Charles Barbier, a former soldier who visited the school.

Barbier told the students about a system of writing he developed. He called his system, made up of patterns of 12 raised dots, "night writing." He created it to allow soldiers to communicate with each other on the battlefield without speaking. Unfortunately, the system was never put to use because it was too difficult for the soldiers to master. But young Louis realized that this system of raised dots could be simplified. He worked at making the system easier to use and eventually came up with what we now know as the Braille system of writing.

The letters of the Braille alphabet are formed from various combinations of six dots. In addition, there are Braille symbols for numbers, punctuation marks, and commonly used groups of letters such as *ch* and *sh*. Braille is read by running the index finger lightly over the lines of raised dots.

Today, Braille has been adapted for use in nearly every written language. When Helen Keller was growing up, however, Braille was only one of several **tactile,** or touch-based, writing systems. Eventually, Helen learned five different systems so she could read as many books as possible.

Chapter THREE

Speaking Out

HELEN KELLER ENTERED RADCLIFFE COLLEGE in 1900. Again, Annie Sullivan was beside her, spelling lectures and books into her hand. At Radcliffe, Keller discovered that she had a talent for writing. One professor said later, "She can write better than any pupil I ever had, man or woman. She has an excellent 'ear' for the flow of sentences." He encouraged her to write a book about her experiences.

Keller set to work on her book. She wrote each chapter in Braille and then typed it for others to read. A young professor from nearby Harvard University helped her polish

Helen Keller was a quick and accurate typist.

her work. His name was John Macy. Her book, *The Story of My Life,* was published in 1903.

John Macy was a socialist. Socialists believe that wealth should be spread evenly among a nation's people. In a truly socialist country, no one would be very rich or very poor. Keller and Sullivan had countless discussions with Macy about the world situation. Macy's ideas had a powerful effect on Keller. She became interested in the conditions of poor people in the United States and around the world. Through her writing, she hoped that she could be of help.

Helen Keller, John Macy, and Annie Sullivan Macy at their home in Wrentham, Massachusetts

In 1905, John Macy and Annie Sullivan were married. He moved into Helen and Annie's home in Wrentham, Massachusetts. Keller wrote articles about the hardships of factory workers and the struggle for woman suffrage, or the right of women to vote. She also wrote on behalf of people who were blind. She insisted that blind people could hold jobs and live meaningful lives. She and Sullivan traveled from city to city, giving public lectures. Keller spoke and Sullivan **interpreted** her speech to the audience.

Helen Keller traveled to many cities and gave lectures. Annie Sullivan helped to interpret her speech for the audience.

People were happy to listen to Helen Keller when she talked about blindness and deafness. The reaction was very different when she spoke of women's rights, poverty, or socialism. Some people said Keller had no right to discuss such things. What did she know about the world, because she couldn't see or hear? People claimed she was only repeating things Sullivan told her. In reality, Sullivan disapproved of Keller's socialist ideas. Keller read widely and exchanged letters with people from all backgrounds. She relied on Sullivan to spell to her and interpret her speech, but her ideas were her own.

From the start, Annie Sullivan and John Macy had an unhappy marriage. Macy left in 1913. Three years later, Sullivan became ill and spent a summer in Puerto Rico to regain her health. For the first time in nearly 30 years, Helen Keller and Annie Sullivan were separated. While Sullivan was away, Keller spent much of her time with a young newspaper reporter named Peter Fagan. Fagan learned to finger spell, and he became Keller's secretary and close friend. When Fagan asked Keller to marry him, she joyfully said yes. Helen's mother was horrified. She did not believe that a deafblind woman should think about marriage and children. Keller's family forced her to break her engagement.

Helen Keller and Annie Sullivan dressed in sequined costumes for their vaudeville performances.

In the years that followed, Keller and Sullivan were hard-pressed for money. In 1920, they turned to well-paid work as **vaudeville** performers. Vaudeville theater presented variety shows with music, dance, and other acts. Keller and Sullivan went on

Interesting Fact

▶ Helen Keller played herself in *Deliverance*, a silent film released in 1919.

21

tours all over the country. As many as three times a day, they described how Keller had learned language with Sullivan as her teacher. Keller enjoyed answering questions from the audience. When people asked her if she could imagine

colors, she said, "No, but sometimes I feel blue, and sometimes I see red."

In 1924, Keller joined the staff of the American Foundation for the Blind in New York. For the next three decades, she traveled the world for the foundation, speaking about the abilities and needs of blind people. She still cared deeply about the struggles of all people, blind and sighted. In her work for the blind, however, she felt she could make the most lasting difference.

VAUDEVILLE SHOWS WERE POPULAR IN THE UNITED States for about 50 years, beginning in the late 1800s. People of all ages packed the theaters to marvel at magicians, dancing bears, jugglers, and gymnasts. Comedians (such as Buster Keaton and his parents, below) made them howl with laughter, and soulful singers moved them to tears. Some shows had as many as 20 acts.

Some people accused Helen Keller and Annie Sullivan of turning Keller's deaf-blindness into a kind of freak show. It seemed beneath their dignity to share vaudeville billing with men who sat on ladies' big hats (above), sword-swallowers, and trained monkeys. Yet vaudeville gave Keller and Sullivan the chance to carry a serious message to the public. Their story told countless people about the true abilities of those who might seem helpless and limited.

Vaudeville died out in the early 1930s. By that time, movies began to include sound, attracting a wider audience. Live variety shows disappeared, replaced by the delights of the silver screen.

Chapter FOUR

Breaking Down the Walls

ON A TRIP TO EUROPE IN 1932, HELEN KELLER and Annie Sullivan received a hero's welcome. They were awarded honorary degrees in Scotland and met the king and queen of England. This was the last major trip Helen Keller and her teacher ever made together. After a series of illnesses, Annie Sullivan died in 1936 at the home she and Keller shared in Forest Hills, New York.

Keller was numb with grief after Sullivan's death. In her journal she wrote, "It seems as if I should **henceforth** tread paths that lead nowhere." As time passed, however, Keller determined to carry on with her work. Polly Thomson, a Scottish woman living in the United States, became her interpreter. Thomson had known Keller since 1914 when she began working for her. As Sullivan became older and sick, Thomson began to take over as Keller's interpreter and companion. Keller continued to travel and lecture until she was almost 80 years old. Between 1946 and 1957, she visited many countries, urging national leaders to open schools for blind children. In Africa, Asia, and Latin America, many schools for the blind were

Polly Thomson (right) took over as Keller's interpreter and companion when Annie Sullivan got sick.

founded as a result of Keller's visits. She also spoke out for world peace, asking international leaders not to use nuclear weapons. The U.S. State Department considered her to be one of the nation's most effective **ambassadors** of goodwill.

After Sullivan died, Keller and Thomson moved to a lovely home called Arcan Ridge near Westport, Connecticut. Keller spent

Interesting Fact

▸ Among Helen Keller's many published works is a long poem called *Song of the Stone Wall.*

Patty Duke met Helen Keller at Arcan Ridge.

many happy days reading in her study, its walls lined with Braille books. The public never lost interest in her life story. She was the subject of the 1955 movie *The Unconquered* (later renamed *Helen Keller in Her Story*). The 1959 Broadway play *The Miracle Worker* was based on Sullivan's early work with Keller in Tuscumbia. *The Miracle Worker* became an award-winning movie in 1962.

Patty Duke, the 12-year-old actress who played Helen on Broadway, met the real Helen Keller at Arcan Ridge. "She was so jolly, like a jolly grandmother," Duke wrote later. "I'd expected serious or sweet, but not jolly." Keller was often serious, because she cared so deeply about the world and its people. She also had a lively sense of humor, and sometimes she was anything but sweet. Helen Keller was her own boss. One of her friends wrote, "Helen is unmanageable. This began with her mother and has continued to this day."

Thomson died in 1960, and Keller remained at Arcan Ridge with a housekeeper. That same year, Keller suffered her first stroke. After this, she wrote letters and received many visitors, but basically she retired from public life. Helen Keller died at her home on June 1, 1968. Her ashes are buried near those of Annie Sullivan and Polly Thomson at the National Cathedral in Washington, D.C.

Helen Keller lived an amazing life. Among her friends were writers, actors, inventors, and heads of state. But she was also a friend to countless blind, deaf, and sighted children. She met 11 U.S.

Helen Keller enjoyed the roses in her backyard at Arcan Ridge.

presidents and traveled the world. Her books, articles, and speeches touched the lives of millions of people.

Wherever she went, Helen Keller carried a message of hope and peace. In words she spoke hundreds of times on the vaudeville stage, "We live by each other and for each other. Alone we can do so little. Together we can do so much. Only love can break down the walls that stand between us and our happiness."

One of Keller's many accomplishments was being awarded an Oscar for the documentary Helen Keller in Her Story.

Time LINE

1887   1896   1960

1880   Helen Keller is born on June 27 in Tuscumbia, Alabama.

1887   Annie Sullivan is sent from the Perkins Institution for the Blind to be Helen's teacher.

1888   Keller enrolls at the Perkins Institution in Boston.

1896   Keller enrolls at the Cambridge School for Young Ladies.

1900   Keller enters Radcliffe College.

1903   *The Story of My Life* is published.

1904   Keller graduates from Radcliffe College.

1918   Keller begins making *Deliverance,* a film based on her life.

1920   With Sullivan, Keller becomes a star of the vaudeville stage.

1924   Keller begins work with the American Foundation for the Blind, speaking about the needs and abilities of blind people.

1929   *Midstream: My Later Life* is published.

1936   Annie Sullivan Macy dies.

1946   The American Foundation for the Overseas Blind sends Keller on the first of a series of visits to other countries.

1959   *The Miracle Worker* opens on Broadway, telling the story of Keller's early childhood.

1960   Polly Thompson dies. Helen Keller suffers her first stroke.

1968   Helen Keller dies on June 1 at her home in Westport, Connecticut.

2003   Helen Keller represents the state of Alabama on a commemorative quarter.

accurate (AK-yuh-ruht)
Something that is accurate contains no mistakes. Helen Keller was an accurate typist.

ambassadors (am-BASS-uh-durs)
Ambassadors are people sent from one country to another to promote peace and understanding. Helen Keller was an ambassador of goodwill who traveled to many foreign countries.

Braille (BRAYL)
Braille is a reading and writing system for blind people based on combinations of dots. Helen Keller learned to read and write Braille.

civilian (si-VIL-yuhn)
A civilian is someone who is not an active member of a police, fire-fighting, or military force. The Presidential Medal of Freedom is the highest honor the United States can give to a civilian.

disabilities (diss-a-BIL-et-ees)
Disabilities are any physical or mental conditions that may limit a person's ability to do certain things. Helen Keller had two disabilities, blindness and deafness.

gravely (GRAYV-lee)
Something that happens gravely is very serious and may cause great harm. Helen Keller became gravely ill as a young child.

henceforth (HENS-forth)
Henceforth is an old-fashioned word meaning from now on. After Annie Sullivan died, Helen Keller felt that henceforth she would walk paths leading nowhere.

imitate (IM-uh-tate)
To imitate someone or something means to copy it. Helen Keller lost her ability to imitate speech when she lost her hearing.

interpreted (in-TUR-prit-ed)
When something is interpreted, it is translated from one language into another. Annie Sullivan interpreted Helen Keller's finger spelling into spoken English.

lectures (LEK-churs)
Lectures are educational talks. Annie Sullivan spelled the teachers' lectures into Helen Keller's hand.

tactile (TAK-tul)
The word tactile refers to anything related to the sense of touch. Braille is a tactile method of reading.

vaudeville (VAWD-vil)
Vaudeville is a form of theater that consists of a number of different act such as comedians, dancers, acrobats, etc. Helen Keller and Annie Sullivan told their story on the vaudeville stage.

For Further INFORMATION

Web Sites

Visit our homepage for lots of links about Helen Keller:
http://www.childsworld.com/links.html

Note to Parents, Teachers, and Librarians:
We routinely verify our Web links to make sure they're safe,
active sites—so encourage your readers to check them out!

Books

Dash, Joan. *The World at Her Fingertips: The Story of Helen Keller.* New York: Scholastic Press, 2001.

Lawlor, Laurie. *Helen Keller: Rebellious Spirit.* New York: Holiday House, 2001.

Sullivan, George. *Helen Keller.* New York: Scholastic, Inc., 2001.

Places to Visit or Contact

Ivy Green
To visit the home where Helen Keller was born
300 West North Commons
Tuscumbia, AL 35674
256/383-4066

Colbert County Tourism and Convention Bureau
To get more information about the town where Helen Keller was born and about the Helen Keller Festival held there each year
P.O. Box 740425
Tuscumbia, AL 35674
800/344-0783

Index

About the Author

DEBORAH KENT GREW UP IN LITTLE FALLS, NEW JERSEY, WHERE SHE WAS THE FIRST TOTALLY BLIND student to attend the local public school. She earned a B.A. in English at Oberlin College and received a master's degree from Smith College School for Social Work. For four years she worked as a social worker at the University Settlement House in New York City.

In 1975, Ms. Kent decided to pursue her lifelong interest in writing. She moved to San Miguel de Allende, Mexico, a town with a thriving community of writers and artists. In San Miguel she completed her first novel for young adults, *Belonging,* based on her experiences as a blind student attending a regular school. Ms. Kent is the author of 18 novels for young adults and more than 50 nonfiction titles for children. She lives in Chicago with her husband, children's author R. Conrad Stein, and their daughter Janna.